35 Santa Patterns for Carvers

Al Streetman

Schiffer Publishing Ltd

Lower Valley Road, Atglen, PA 19310 USA

ACKNOWLEDGMENTS

The following people helped make this book possible. I thank you all.

Tim and Debbie Effrem, Woodcarvers Supply, Inc. (1-800-284-6229): For graciously providing the excellent quality tools I am using on my current projects. They carry an outstanding assortment of fine carving tools, supplies, and books.

DecoArt: The paint samples were excellent, and satisfactory in all respects.

Royal Brush Mfg., Inc.: High quality paintbrushes at an affordable price.

David Mather, Tuckaway Timber (603-795-4534): The best basswood and white pine I have found for carving, and very reasonable prices.

Designed by John P. Cheek
Cover design by Bruce M. Waters
Type set in Korinna BT/Korinna BT

ISBN: 0-7643-1657-5
Printed in China

Published by Schiffer Publishing Ltd.
4880 Lower Valley Road
Atglen, PA 19310
Phone: (610) 593-1777; Fax: (610) 593-2002
E-mail: Schifferbk@aol.com
Please visit our web site catalog at
www.schifferbooks.com
We are always looking for people to write books on new and related subjects. If you have an idea for a book please contact us at the above address.

This book may be purchased from the publisher.
Include $3.95 for shipping.
Please try your bookstore first.
You may write for a free catalog.

In Europe, Schiffer books are distributed by
Bushwood Books
6 Marksbury Ave.
Kew Gardens
Surrey TW9 4JF England
Phone: 44 (0) 20 8392-8585; Fax: 44 (0) 20 8392-9876
E-mail: Bushwd@aol.com
Free postage in the U.K., Europe; air mail at cost.

CONTENTS

INTRODUCTION

In response to numerous letters, e-mail, and conversations I have had with many of you, I have raided my pattern vault and put together another pattern book for those of you who want to carve some more Santas. This book does not include a step-by-step carving project, because as the title says, it is a "pattern" book. I do have a selection of various carving books available from the publisher, which feature step-by-step projects as part of their content, if you are new to carving and need more direction than that provided by the patterns and gallery. This book is written more for the carver who has some level of experience, but just needs some basic line drawings/patterns to get started. I will, however, offer some general tips and recommendations as to wood selection, paint colors, and tools. The final choice is, of course, up to you. Some of the patterns shown in the book will appear as real carvings in the photo gallery, so you will have 3-D models to look at in addition to the line drawings. I have submitted the patterns full-size to the publisher, but at times space and page restrictions require them to reduce the size of some of the patterns. If that happens, there will be a note somewhere on the page indicating how much enlargement will be needed to bring the pattern back to full size. Everything on each pattern is drawn in scale to the other pieces, so if you choose to enlarge or reduce the pattern size for your particular needs, it will all still be in proportion to the other pieces.

On the patterns, you will notice an arrow with a "G" superimposed over it. This arrow indicates the recommended grain direction of the wood in relation to the pattern, in order to make carving that particular piece as easy as possible.

I use Basswood whenever possible, but any soft wood such as Jelutong, clear Spruce, or Sugar/White Pine will work equally well. Try to avoid wood that has a lot of knots and burls in it. Trying to carve around and through them, is just going to frustrate you. If possible, use a bandsaw with a 1/8" or 3/16" blade to cut out the pattern pieces. The bandsaw will allow you to release the rough version of the pattern from the block of wood faster than trying to use a coping saw or other means to cut out the pattern.

Recently, I have been using tools (knives and gouges), which are available from Wood Carvers Supply in Englewood, Florida. They are high-quality tools, and very reasonably priced. If you are new to wood carving, they will work with you on the phone to get you set up with the proper tools you need to get the job done.

GENERAL NOTES

1. Trace the pattern pieces or make a copy of them on a photocopying machine. Glue the pattern you copied or traced onto some heavy paper such as poster paper or a manila file folder. When the glue is dry, cut out the pattern. This method will prevent you from ruining the master patterns in your book.

2. Lay your pattern on the wood, trace the outline of it, and saw it out. *Pay close attention to any recommended grain directions indicated on the pattern pieces!!*

3. You should now have a rough blank ready to be carved.

4. Use your own techniques and style to bring the carving to the finished stage.

CARVING TOOLS

If you are already an experienced carver, then most likely you have some favorite tools that you prefer to use in order to achieve the desired results and effects. The variety and multitude of carving tools and accessories available in different stores and catalogs sometimes overwhelm new carvers. Before you go out and take a second mortgage on the ranch just to finance all the tools you "think" you will need to get the job accomplished, try this approach: purchase a fixed-blade bench knife (fairly long wooden handle with about a 1-1/2" long blade), a couple of "V" gouges (perhaps 1/8" and 1/4"), and a couple of "U" gouges. Learn how to sharpen them, because they do not normally come ready to use, no matter what the catalogs may say. Dull knives and gouges are one of the leading causes of frustration for new carvers, because they haven't realized yet that the dullness of their tools is causing the problem. This is the point that some would-be great carvers give up and move on to needlepoint or something else less intimidating. There are many good books on the market that will tell you in words, and show you with photos, how to get the proper edge on the various types of knives and gouges.

Once you have learned how to put a good edge on your tools, maintaining that edge will then only require a mild stropping. You will, of course, have to put the tool on a sharpening stone occasionally, but unless you have dropped the tool or otherwise damaged the edge, most of the time a light stropping will be all that is required.

Once your tools are sharp, create your carving and look at the effects the "V" gouge and the "U" gouge can create. You'll want to add the type that best suits your likes to your tool arsenal.

I use a "V" gouge to outline areas where I want to remove wood, and to create things such as soles on shoes, but personally I find that I use the "U" type gouges much more frequently. Their effect on areas such as hair and beards suits me more than the effect achieved by "V" gouges. You may feel that the "V" does a better job for you, and that is your right. There is no "correct" tool to use, except the one that gives the effect that makes you the happiest. It's all a part of the personal "style" that you have or that you will develop.

TIPS

1. Eyes

A. **QUILT PIN METHOD:** I sometimes use various sizes of plastic-head quilting pins to make eyes. Mark the spot where you want the eyes to be on the finished carving. Using a drill and bit that is slightly larger than the pinhead you are going to use, make a hole for each eye.

Using wire cutters, snip off the pinhead, leaving about 1/4" of the pin attached to the head.

Insert the pinhead into the eye socket, with the pin end going in first. Use a nail set to seat the head into the hole until only a small orb protrudes. This gives a fairly realistic eye without much effort on your part. For extra detail, remove a triangular-shaped piece of wood from the sides of the pinhead. This will make a very realistic eye when it is painted.

B. **PUNCH METHOD:** A second easy way to create eyes is to use carver's eye punches. Select the size eye punch you want to use, based on the size of the eye sockets you have made. Push the eye punch against the socket firmly and rotate it. After making both eyes, remove triangular-shaped pieces of wood from the corners to give more detail. Use your knife, if necessary, to smooth and round off the eyeball.

C. **FOOTBALL METHOD:** A more realistic way to make eyes is to begin by carving the eye sockets so that about a 90 degree angle is formed. Lightly sketch in a football-shaped eye in each socket, such that the top half of the football is on the upper half of the socket, and the lower half of the football is on the lower half of the socket. When you sketch in the footballs, make the outside ends lower than the inside ends. Using the tip of your knife, score the football outline to a depth of about 1/16". Now use the tip of your knife to remove triangular-shaped pieces of wood from the left and right corner of each eye. This will leave a small section of wood inside each football, which will be the eyeball. Use your knife to round off and smooth the eyeball. You can vary the way you remove the triangular-shaped corners, if you want the eyes to be looking more to one side, rather than straight ahead.

D. **MOUND METHOD:** The most realistic way to make eyes is to first rough carve the nose so it is standing out from the face. Next, sketch a circle or oval on each side of the nose to represent where the eye mounds will be located. Using a smaller "V" gouge, such as a 1/8" size, or your knife tip, go around the circles or ovals so the mounds will be defined and separated from the face area. Use your knife to round the sharp edges of the mounds, and the face area around the mounds.

Divide the mounds into thirds by sketching two curved horizontal lines across each one, making sure that the lines join at each corner of the mound. (Look at your own eyes in a mirror to see what I mean here). Using your knife tip, score each horizontal line about 1/16" deep. Working from the **center** of the eye mound, use your knife tip to shave **upward** toward the top horizontal line, and **downward** toward the bottom horizontal line. This will make the eyelids stand out from the eyeball area. Finally, remove small triangular pieces of wood from each corner of the eye, so the eyeball will be rounded from left to right, as well as top to bottom.

Changing the size and shape of the mounds, and the spacing between the horizontal lines, will allow you to achieve many effects and expressions on your carvings.

One last thing concerning eyes: Don't get upset if you discover that you have carved one eye smaller or at a different angle than the other eye. This "accident" may work to your advantage. It will lend an interesting variation to the carving, and no one has to know you didn't do it that way on purpose!!

2. Buying Wood

When buying wood, whether it is Basswood, Spruce, or some other type, try to pick the **lightest** pieces. They tend to have less fat and sap in them, so they are **easier** to carve. I have been obtaining my basswood and white pine from Tuckaway Timber Company (see the acknowledgments in the front of the book). Their wood is fantastic for carving, and priced right.

3. Wrinkles and Folds

An easy way to determine where you want to place some wrinkles and folds in the arms, torso and legs is to observe and note where the wood grain changes direction as you are carving. Usually in the crook of an elbow or behind the knees, you will notice that wood "fuzzies" try to appear, no matter how carefully you carve or how sharp your knife is. That is because the wood grain direction is changing, and in one direction or the other, you are trying to carve against the grain, thus the "fuzzies" appear. These spots are perfect candidates for wrinkles and folds, made with a large "V" tool or by cutting wedges out with your knife. As a beginning carver, if you do nothing more than add a few cuts in these areas, you will be amazed at the difference in the way the carving looks. With experience, you will start noticing other places to add wrinkles and folds.

4. Enlarging or Reducing Patterns

For those of you who have never had much practice enlarging or reducing patterns, or being able to calculate how much enlargement or reduction you need to select on the photocopying machine, here are some general guidelines:

Let's say you have a pattern that shows a side profile requiring 2" thick wood, and you want to make the pattern larger so it will fit on 3" thick wood. Use the following formula to calculate what percentage enlargement to select on the copier:

[New Dimension Desired ÷ Present Dimension] x 100 = % to select on copier machine. Using our example, this would work out as follows:

[3" ÷ 2"] x 100 = **150%** .

Going the other way, let's say you have a pattern that shows a 2" side profile, and you want to reduce it down so it will fit on a piece of 1-3/4" thick wood. Using the same formula, it works out as follows:

[1.75" ÷ 2"] x 100 = **87.5 %** .

If the machine you are using won't go large enough or small enough to get the job done on the first try, additional steps may be required. Go ahead and make your first copy using the largest enlargement or reduction setting you can select. Measure the **new** dimensions on your **copy, (which will now be your Present Dimension)**, then use the same formula as before to calculate how much additional enlargement or reduction is needed to get the pattern to the size you desired it to be.

5. Holding Hands

When making separate hands that are going to be holding some object, it is easiest if you first cut out the top profile of the hand, drill a hole large enough for the object to fit through, then saw out the side profile of the hand. This procedure will help prevent the hand from splitting when you drill it.

6. Carving Hands Separately

For those patterns where the hands are to be carved separately, the following instructions may be used if you are not familiar with this method of hand carving:

(A) Lay out the top view of the hands on a piece of 3/4" thick basswood. Leave a short section of wood at the rear of each hand when you lay out the pattern. This section will serve as a handle while you carve and shape the hands, and will form the wrist pegs in a later step. Saw out the top profile of the hands. (A scroll saw or bandsaw with a 1/8" wide blade works great for this).

(B) Now sketch in the side profile of the hands, then saw them out. You now should have two hands that will require very little work to finish.

(C) Sketch in the thumbs. Remove wood from each hand using a knife, so the thumbs are well defined, then round off the sharp edges of the thumbs.

(D) Draw a line in the middle of the finger section to divide it in half. Now draw lines to divide each of these sections in half. You should now have four fingers defined, all approximately equal.

(E) Using a **1/8" "V" gouge**, go over these lines so the fingers will be separated. As an option, to add further detail without too much pain on your part, use a bandsaw, scroll saw, or coping saw to carefully saw along these lines. Use your knife to remove any fuzzy wood caused by the saw cuts, and to remove any sharp edges still remaining on the hands. At this point, if you do nothing else, you will have two hands that will look perfectly good once they are painted. Experienced carvers may add more detailing as they desire, such as knuckles and wrinkles on the finger joints.

(F) Using your knife, trim down the sections of wood protruding from the rear of the hands, so as to form a "wrist" or "pin" that will fit snugly into the holes drilled in the arms. When done properly, the hand should appear to be coming out of the sleeve. This method allows you to turn the hands in various directions, so your carvings will appear more lifelike.

SPECIAL TIPS FOR SANTAS

1. For realistic fur, I use a product made by DecoArt called "Snowtex." This is a white, grainy acrylic mixture that you apply with a small flat brush. After it is dry and painted, it gives a very good fur look.

2. If you don't want to try carving the "pom-pom" ball on Santa's hat, you can make one the easy way by using unpainted wooden beads which can be obtained at most craft stores. Buy various sizes, then use one which best fits the hat, after the head and hat are carved. Carve a flat spot on the hat, and glue the bead to it. If the bead has a hole in it, fill the hole with wood filler after the glue dries. An alternate choice is to drill a 1/8" hole into the hat, about 1/4" deep. Insert (glue) a short section of 1/8" wooden dowel into the hole. Put a small drop of glue on the end of the dowel and slide the bead onto the dowel until it is flush against the hat. When the glue is dry, use your knife to trim off any excess wood protruding from the bead. This method is the most realistic one I have found for making the pom-poms.

3. If you want to make one of your Santas patriotic, an easy way to make stars on flags and coats is to take a stylus or toothpick and put a dot of White paint where you want the star to be. Starting inside the dot, while the paint is still wet, drag the tip of the stylus or toothpick toward the edge and out to make a line. Do this for all five points of the star. The bigger you make the dot of paint to begin with, and the further you drag each line outside of the dot, the bigger the star will be.

GENERAL PAINTING SUGGESTIONS

I have included *suggested* colors and paintbrush types and sizes. If you have a preference for a different color scheme or different type of paintbrush, by all means use it.

I have also listed some suggested colors produced by DecoArt and their identification numbers, which I have found to be suitable for painting my carvings. I have used these colors, and the results were excellent. I hope this will help minimize your confusion when trying to sort through the maze of paint brands and colors at your hobby or craft store.

The Royal Brush Mfg. Company makes the best paintbrushes I have found, for the money. They come in a wide assortment of sizes and shapes, are durable, and most important are affordable. In general, here are the ones I use and recommend for painting your carvings.

Royal Golden Taklon series 250 Round, size 0 and 00: Details such as eyes and other small areas.
Royal Golden Taklon series 170 Cat's Tongue, size 2 and 4: Large areas.
Royal Golden Taklon series 150 Short Shader, size 2 and 4: Blending colors. (For example, when blending a "blush" color into the flesh color on faces, hands, etc.)

You may have heard and read this a million times, but when painting your carvings, keep the word *THIN* in mind. What you want to do is stain the wood to give it some color and life, but you don't want the paint so thick that it covers up the beauty of the wood. *NOTE*: When painting faces and hair, I generally use a little thicker mixture of paint than I use on the rest of the carving. I want the face to be a bit more intense than the rest of the carving, since the head and face are what set most of the mood for the carving.

Suggested Colors

General Colors
Titanium White #DA1 (Eyes, highlights in eyes, beards and hair)
Buttermilk #DA3 (Fur on coat)
French Vanilla #DA184 (Fur on coat)
Sand #DA4 (Fur on coat)
Lamp Black #DA67 (Eye dots, boots, mittens, belts)
Burnt Sienna #DA63 (Boots, belts)
Fleshtone #DA78 (Face, hands, other skin areas)
Blush Flesh #DA110 ('Blushing' on cheeks and lips to give a "windburned" effect)
Baby Blue #DA42 (Eye dots)
Camel #DA191(Bags)
Sable Brown #DA61 (Bags)
Venetian Gold #DA72 (Belt buckles)

Coat/Robe colors:
Santa Red #DA170
Lavender #DA34
True Blue #DA36
Napthol Red #DA104
Plum #DA175
Olive Green #DA56
Holly Green #DA48
Olde Gold #DA176
Calico Red #DA20
Reindeer Moss Green #DA187

"Antiquing":
Oak Antiquing Gel #DS30 (Use to give some "age" to the finished carving)
Clear Satin Varnish #DS15 (Use to seal the carving after the antiquing has been done)

If you cannot find these colors locally, you can contact DecoArt at: (http://www.decoart.com). They will be glad to tell you where a dealer is located close to you, and in many cases will provide you with samples of some of the colors for you to try.

Remember: These are only a few of the many colors you can use for your carvings. Should you have other color preferences, use them. Don't be afraid to get wild and experiment with all sorts of color combinations. For those of you (like me), who have difficulty trying to decide which colors work well together, most hobby and art supply stores sell inexpensive color wheels which will show you colors that work together, and colors that oppose each other. I have listed a few combinations here, for illustrative purposes:

MAIN COLOR	CONTRAST COLOR
Red	Green
Orange	Blue
Yellow	Violet

A good color wheel will not only show you main and contrast colors, it will also show colors that blend.

"ANTIQUING" the PROJECT

Once the paint is dry, you may want to "age" your carving with an antiquing product in order to help tone down the colors a bit. I have had excellent results using antiquing gels made by DecoArt. These are available at hobby and craft stores. They come in various colors, so you can create different effects.

Brush a coat of antiquing gel on the wood, then wipe it off using a damp rag or sponge. It is your option how much you wipe off. After the antiquing is dry, I like to finish my carvings with a coat of brush-on acrylic varnish. DecoArt also makes an excellent varnish. I prefer the one that leaves a satin finish. This particular finish is not too flat or too glossy, but leaves a "soft" look to the completed carving. (I usually put a coat of varnish on the face, hand, and other flesh areas BEFORE I antique the carving). This will prevent these areas from absorbing too much antiquing color.

If there is something you would like to discuss personally with me, please feel free to contact me at:

Al Streetman
402 North Broad Street
Guthrie, Oklahoma 73044
(405) 282-8234

or by e-mail at: astreetman@mmcable.com

I promise not to bite or growl, and I'm always receptive to comments and new ideas.

GALLERY AND STUDY MODELS

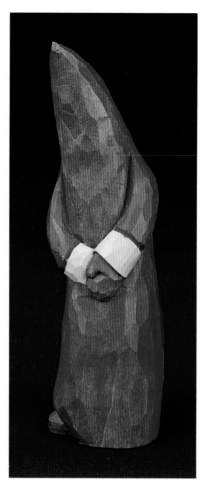

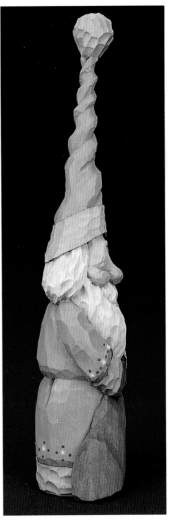

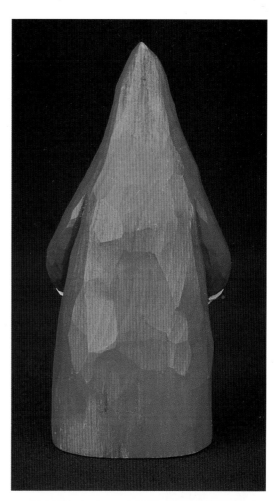

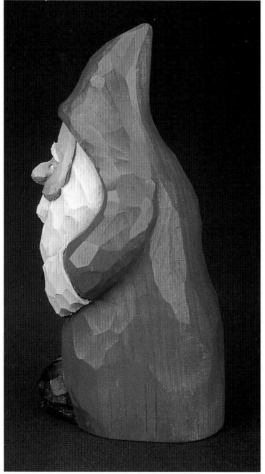

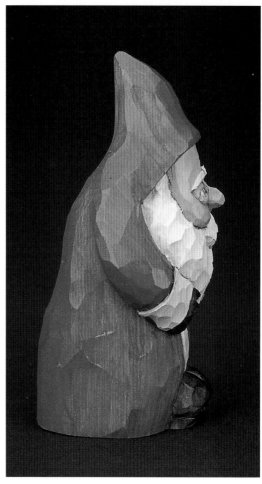

PATTERNS

Walking stick is made from a piece of scrap wood or a twig.

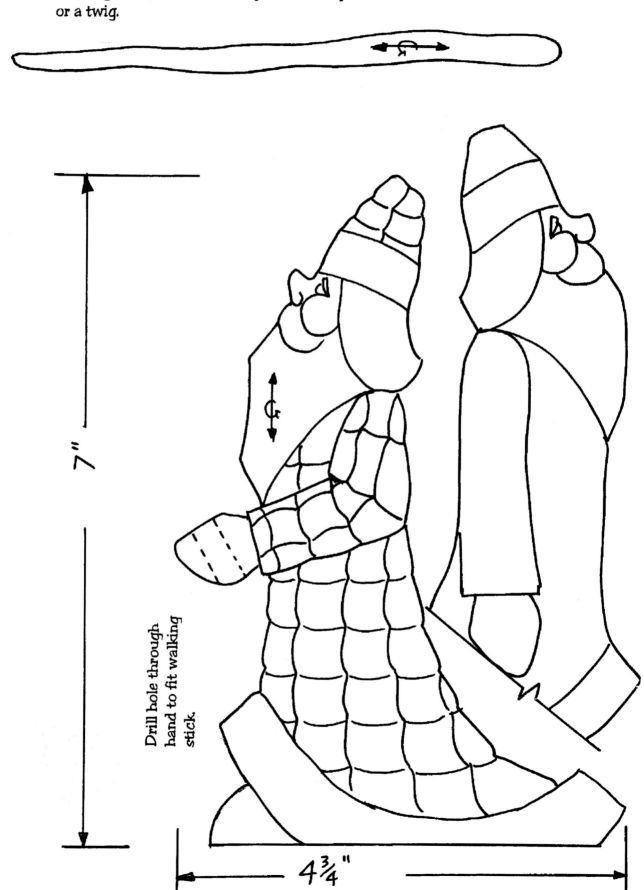

7"

Drill hole through hand to fit walking stick.

4¾"

Walking stick is made from scrap wood or a twig.

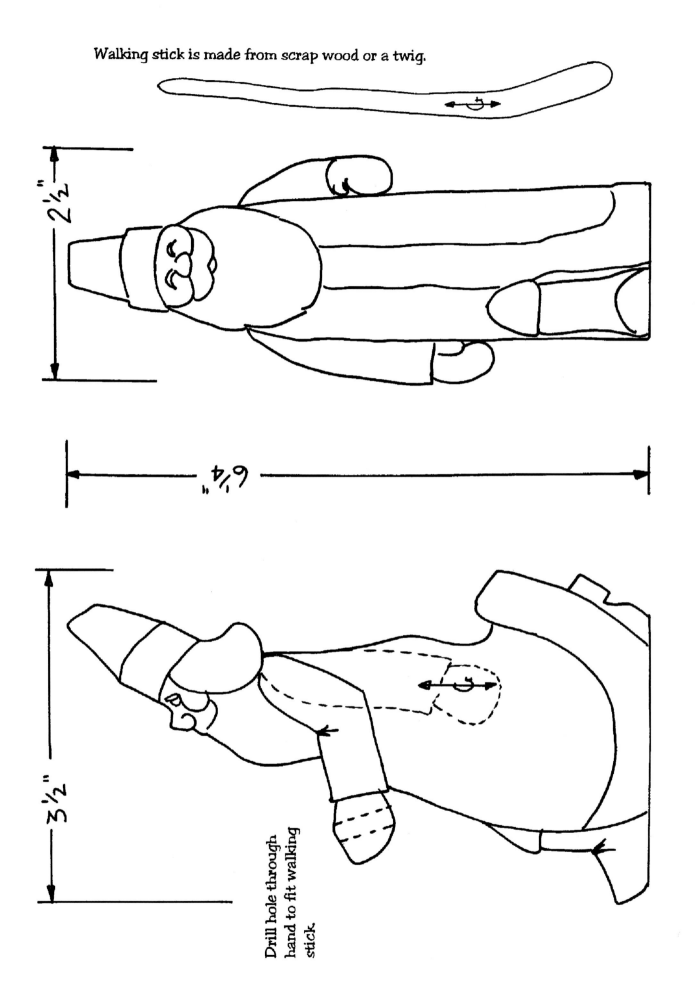

2½"

6¼"

3½"

Drill hole through hand to fit walking stick.

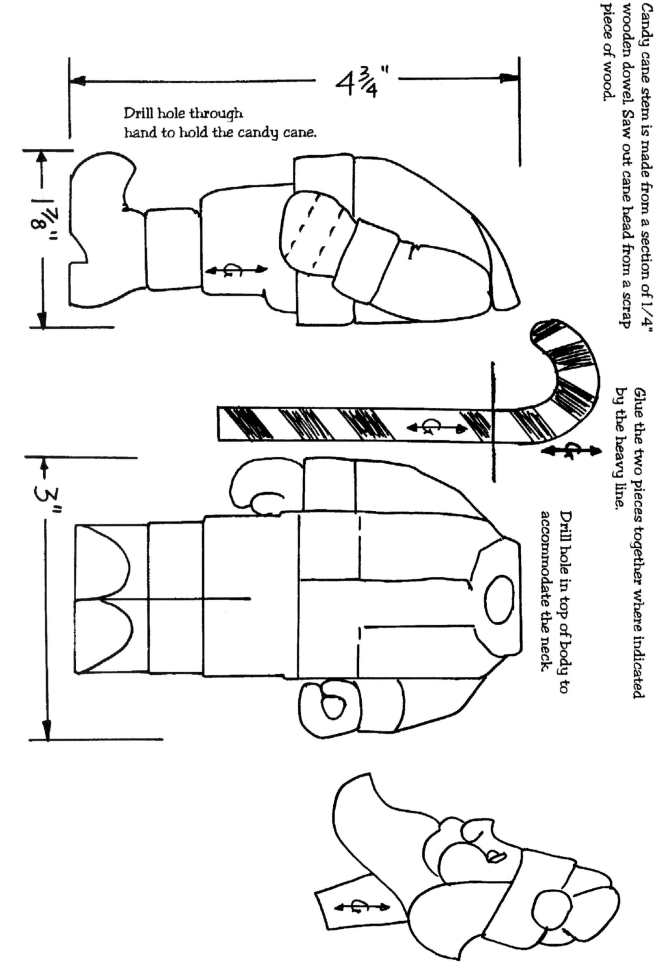

Candy cane stem is made from a section of 1/4" wooden dowel. Saw out cane head from a scrap piece of wood.

4¾"

Drill hole through hand to hold the candy cane.

1⅞"

Glue the two pieces together where indicated by the heavy line.

3"

Drill hole in top of body to accommodate the neck.

Saw plug and about 8 lights from scrap wood. Drill 1/16" holes in them as indicated by dotted lines.

7"

2"

2¾"

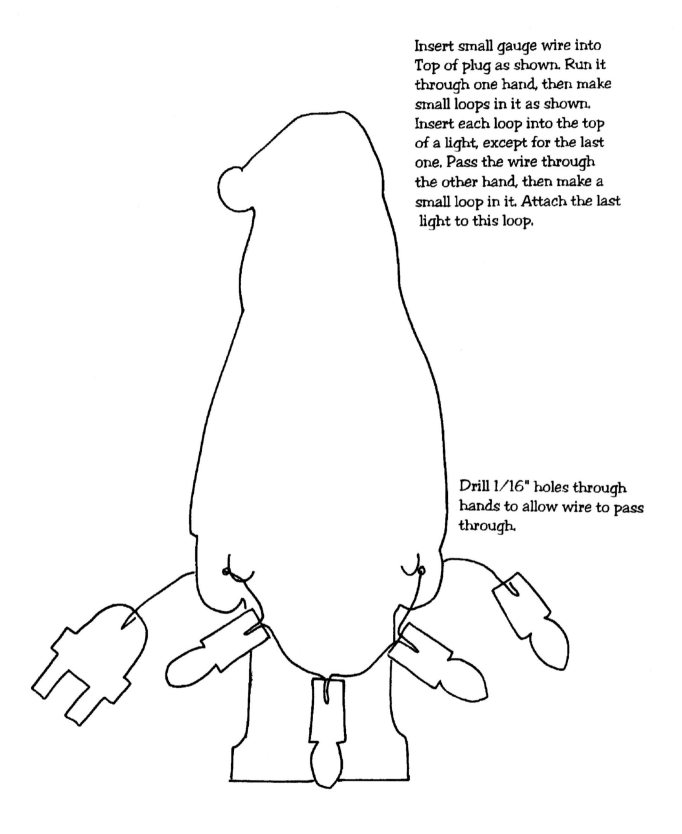

Insert small gauge wire into
Top of plug as shown. Run it
through one hand, then make
small loops in it as shown.
Insert each loop into the top
of a light, except for the last
one. Pass the wire through
the other hand, then make a
small loop in it. Attach the last
light to this loop.

Drill 1/16" holes through
hands to allow wire to pass
through.

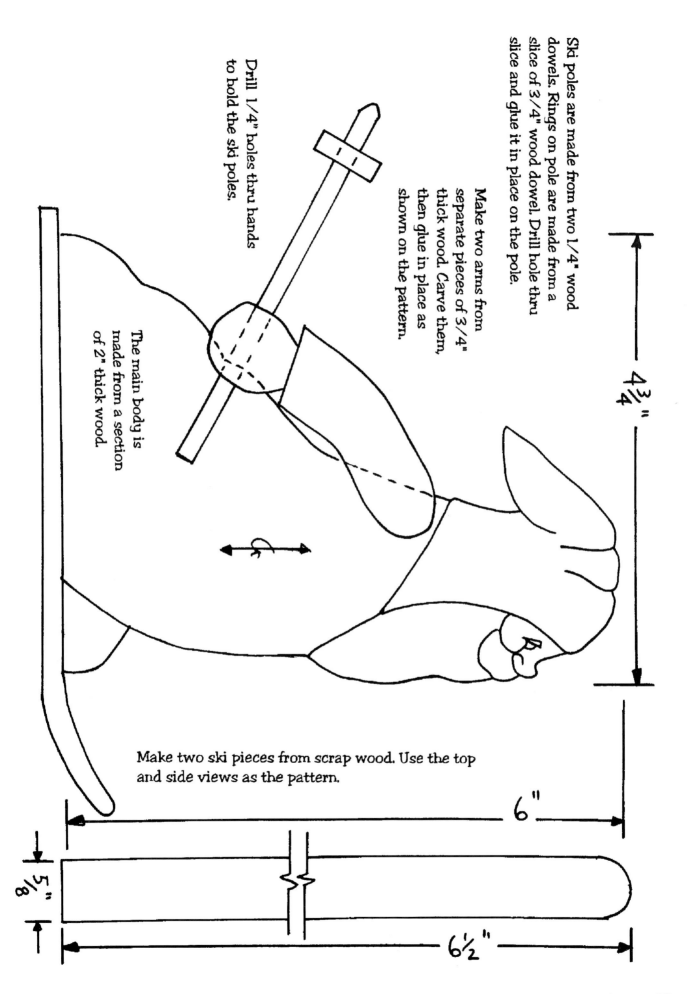

Ski poles are made from two 1/4" wood dowels. Rings on pole are made from a slice of 3/4" wood dowel. Drill hole thru slice and glue it in place on the pole.

Make two arms from separate pieces of 3/4" thick wood. Carve them, then glue in place as shown on the pattern.

Drill 1/4" holes thru hands to hold the ski poles.

The main body is made from a section of 2" thick wood.

Make two ski pieces from scrap wood. Use the top and side views as the pattern.

4¾"

6"

5⁄8"

6½"

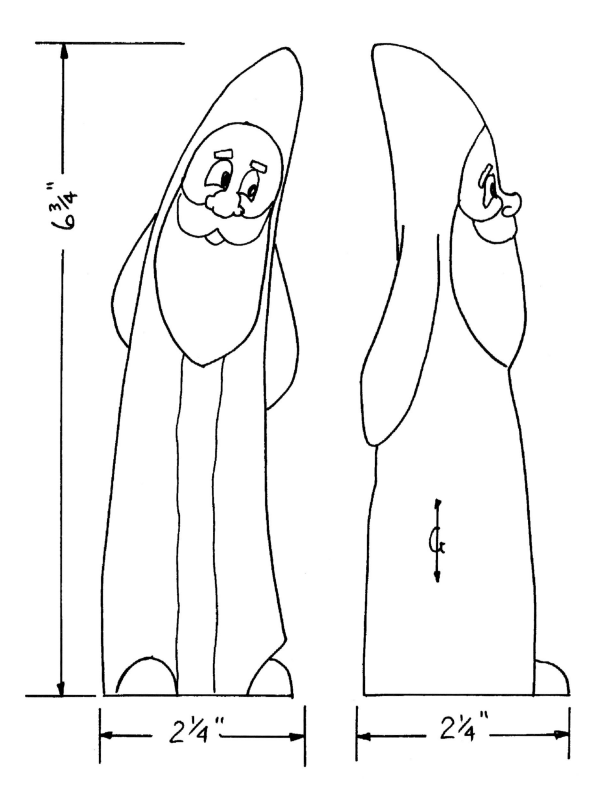

6 ¾"

2 ¼"

2 ¼"

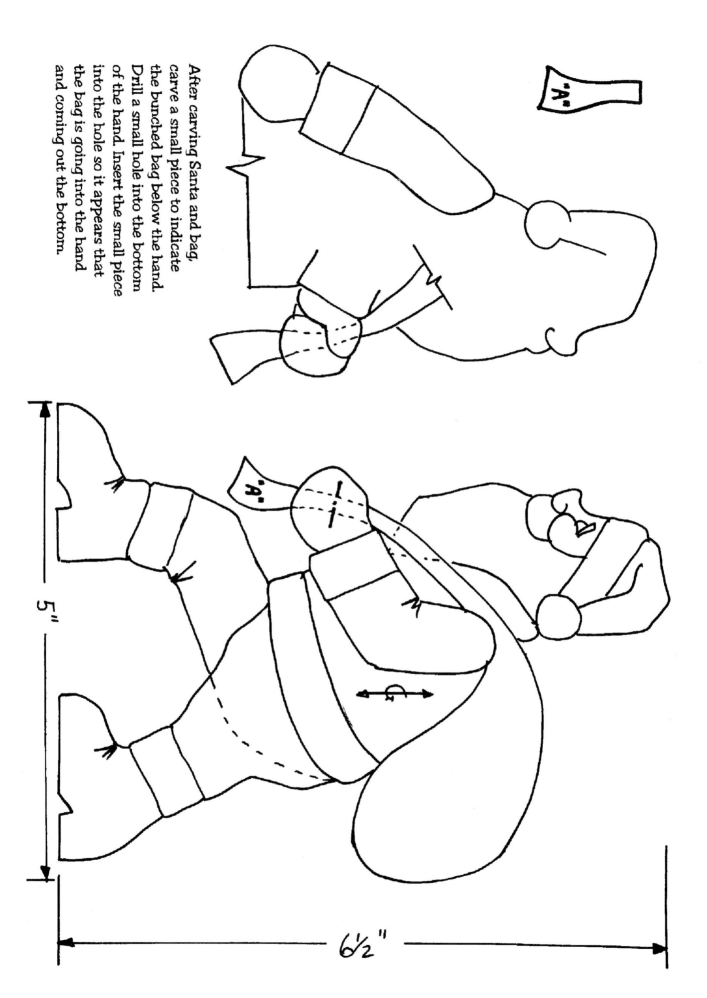

After carving Santa and bag,
carve a small piece to indicate
the bunched bag below the hand.
Drill a small hole into the bottom
of the hand. Insert the small piece
into the hole so it appears that
the bag is going into the hand
and coming out the bottom.

"A"

5"

6½"

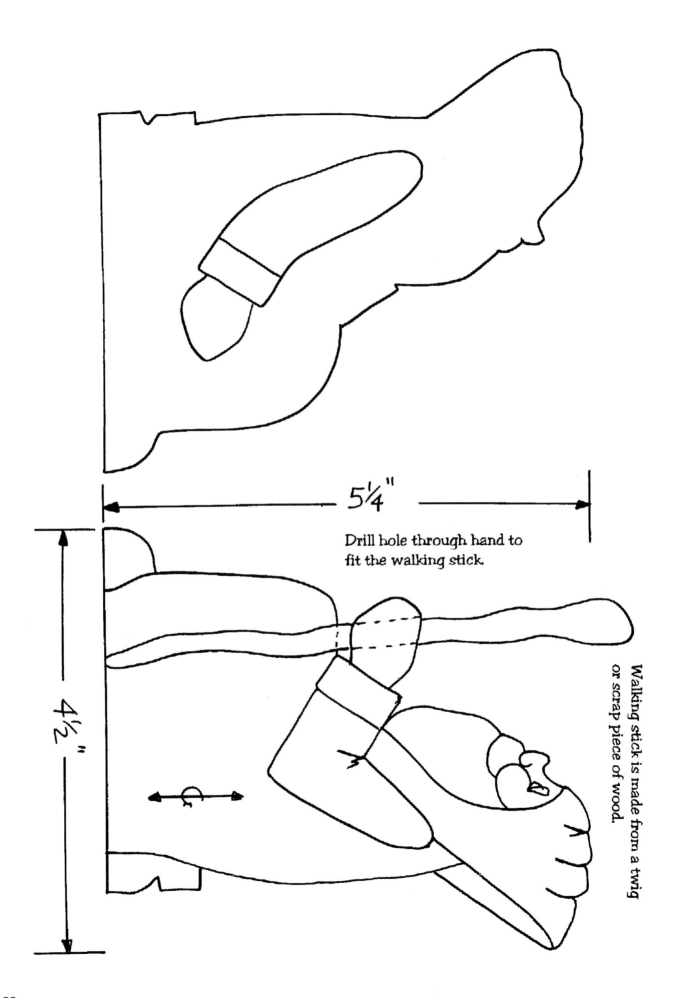

5¼"

Drill hole through hand to fit the walking stick.

4½"

Walking stick is made from a twig or scrap piece of wood.

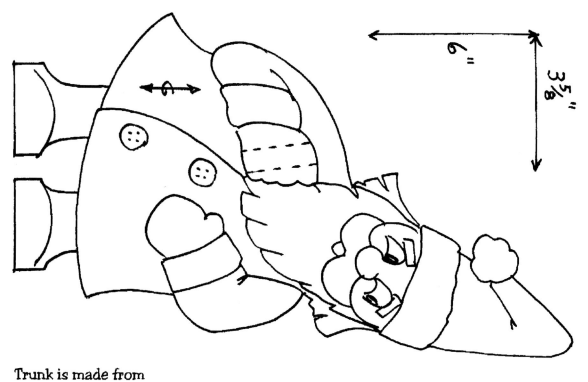

6"

3⅝"

Trunk is made from
a 1/4" wooden dowel.

Tree is made from
scrap wood.

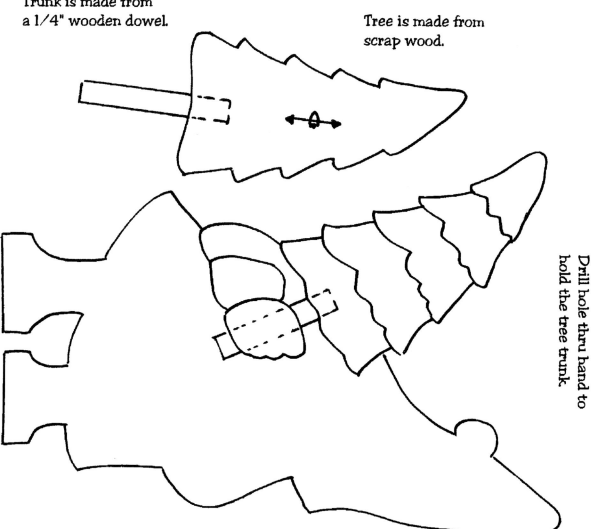

Drill hole thru hand to
hold the tree trunk

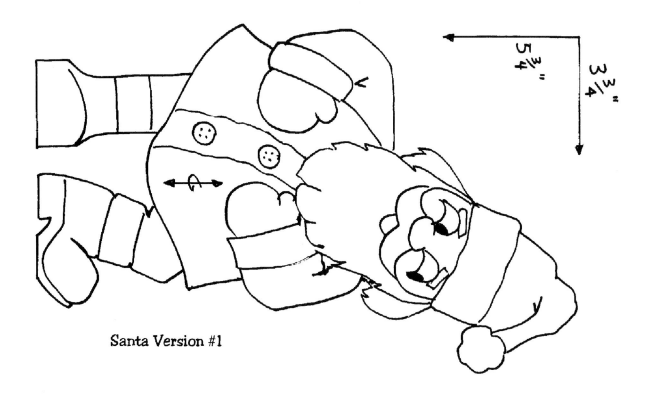

Santa Version #1

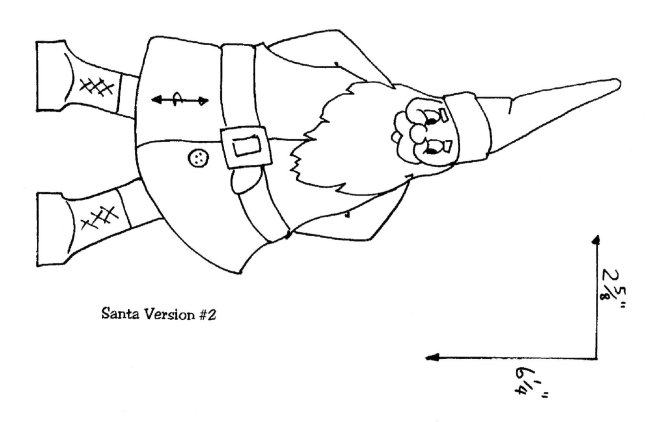

Santa Version #2

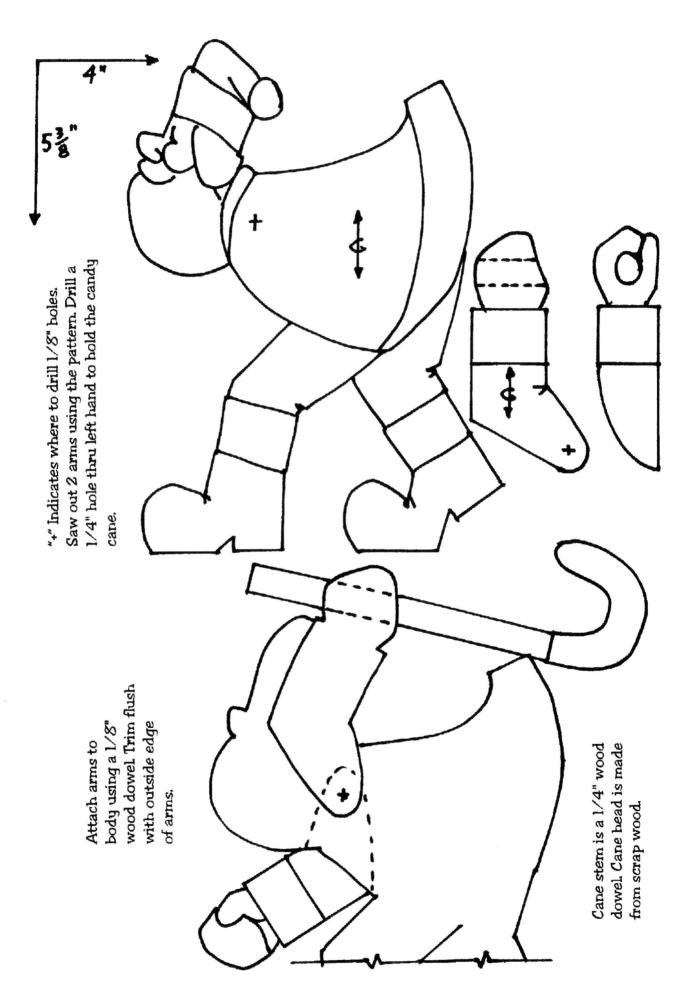

4"

5 3/8"

"+" Indicates where to drill 1/8" holes. Saw out 2 arms using the pattern. Drill a 1/4" hole thru left hand to hold the candy cane.

Attach arms to body using a 1/8" wood dowel Trim flush with outside edge of arms.

Cane stem is a 1/4" wood dowel. Cane head is made from scrap wood.

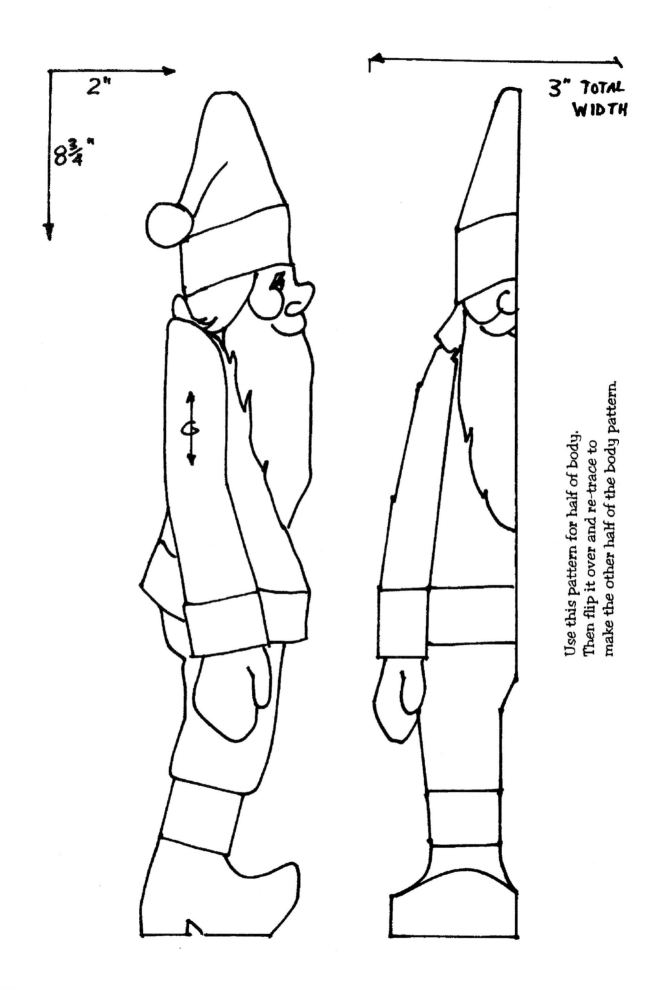

2"

$8\frac{3}{4}$"

3" TOTAL WIDTH

Use this pattern for half of body.
Then flip it over and re-trace to
make the other half of the body pattern.

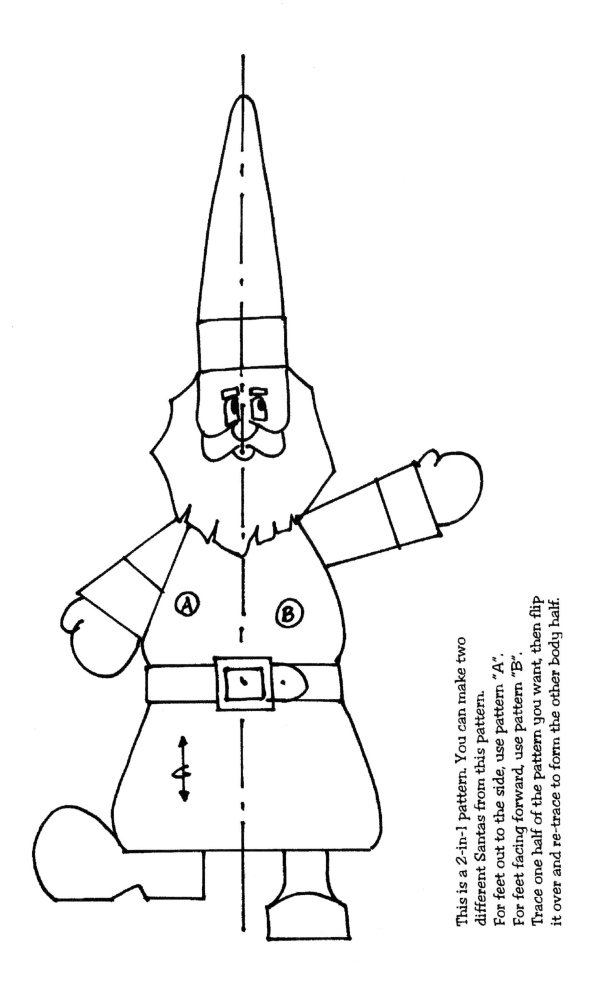

This is a 2-in-1 pattern. You can make two different Santas from this pattern.
For feet out to the side, use pattern "A".
For feet facing forward, use pattern "B".
Trace one half of the pattern you want, then flip it over and re-trace to form the other body half.

8"

4⅛"

8½"

3½"

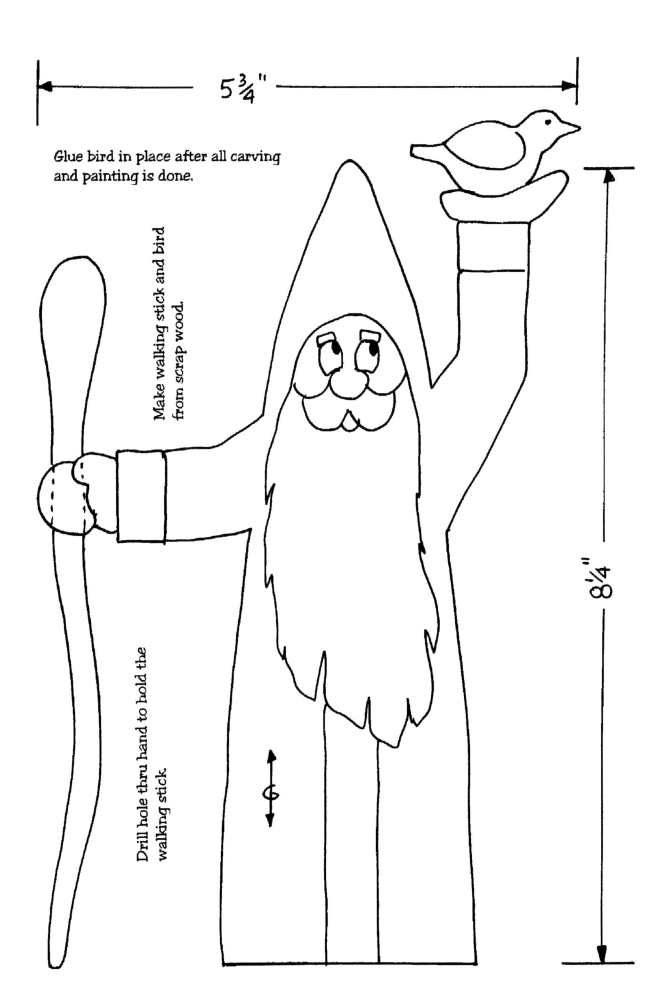

5 ¾"

Glue bird in place after all carving and painting is done.

Make walking stick and bird from scrap wood.

Drill hole thru hand to hold the walking stick.

8 ¼"

3½"

6"

9"

3½"

9"

7"

3⅝"

G

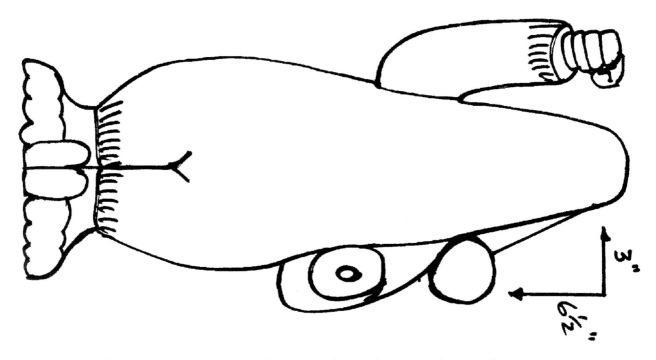

Use hand pattern shown here for the left hand. Place object of your choice in the hand.

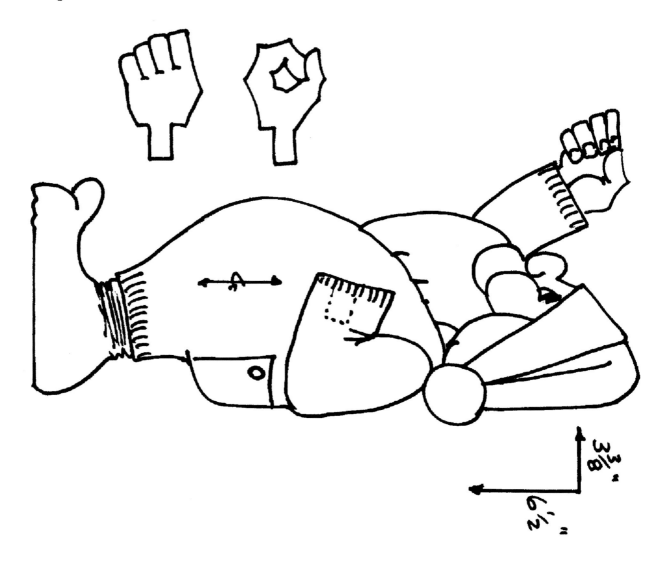

Right hand can be used to hold an object of your choice,
such as a tree or candy cane. Drill an appropriately-sized
hole thru the hand for whatever object you choose.

Candy cane shown here is made from scrap wood pieces.

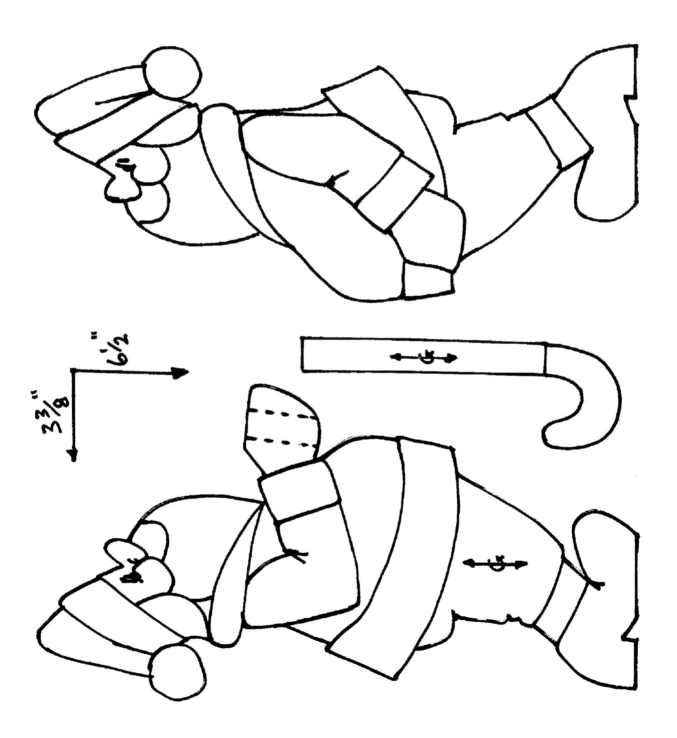

3⅛"

2⅛"

8"

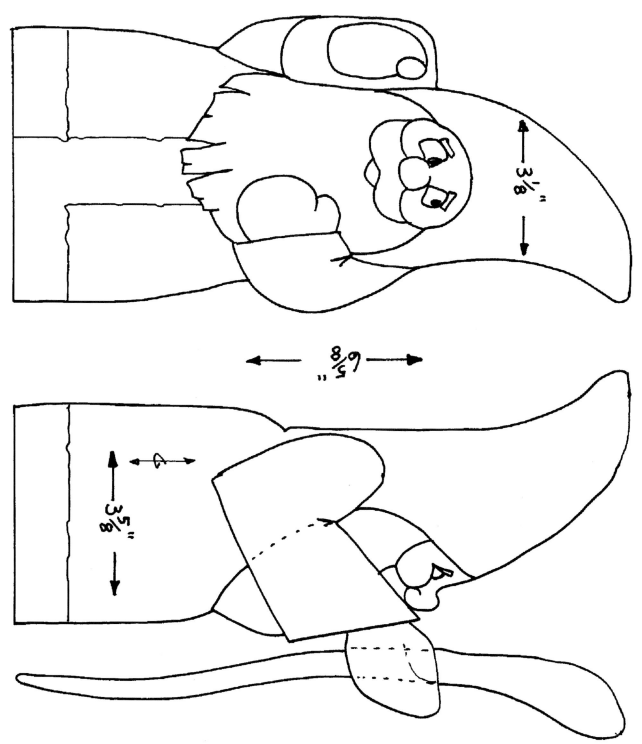

Walking stick is made from scrap wood.
Drill hole thru hand to hold the walking stick.

3 7/8

4 3/4

4 3/4 "

6 1/4 "

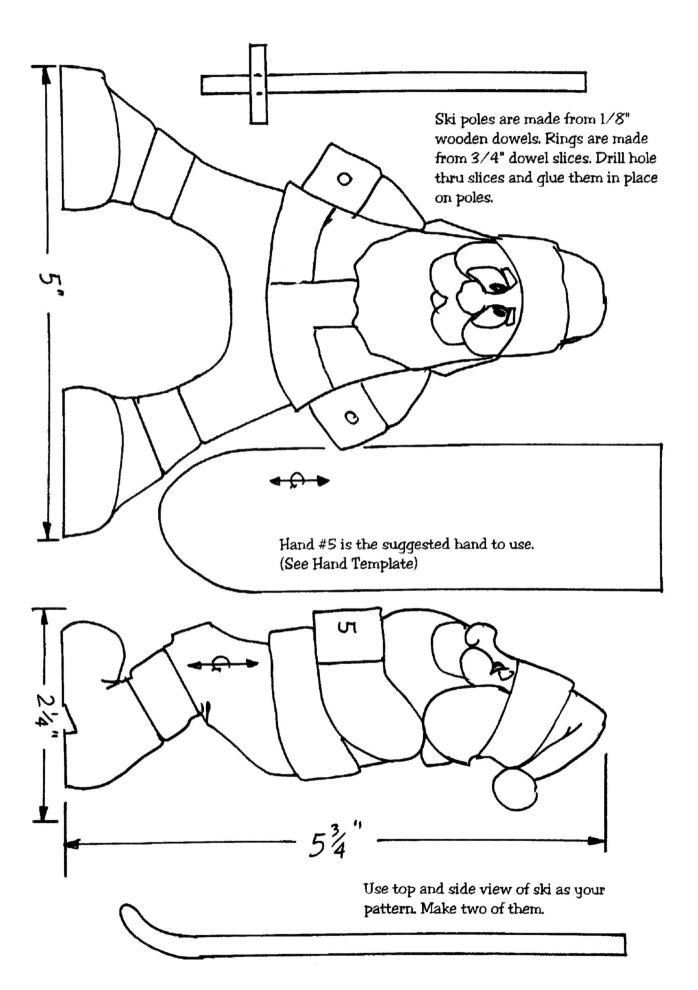

Ski poles are made from 1/8"
wooden dowels. Rings are made
from 3/4" dowel slices. Drill hole
thru slices and glue them in place
on poles.

Hand #5 is the suggested hand to use.
(See Hand Template)

5"

2¼"

5¾"

5

Use top and side view of ski as your
pattern. Make two of them.

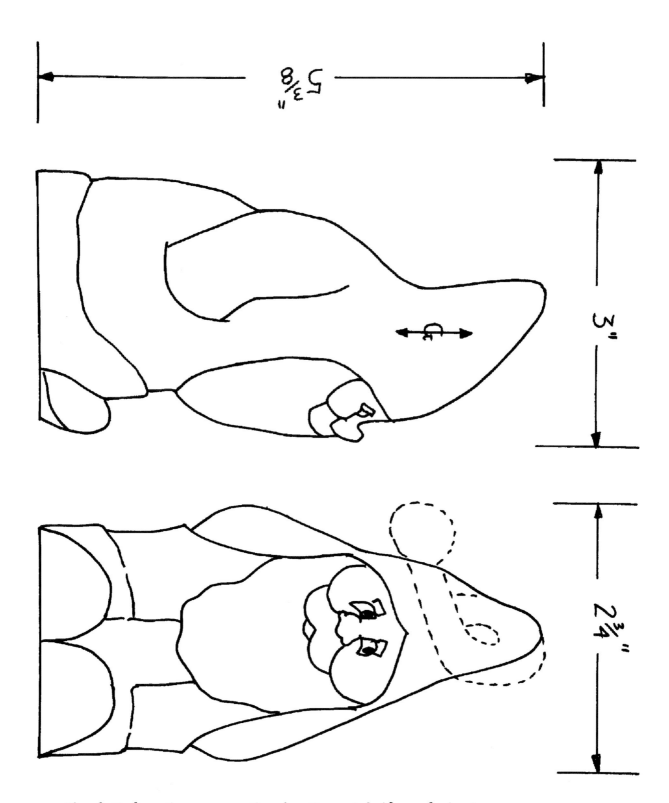

Use dotted section as an optional pattern style if you desire to carve the hood with the curly-cue swirl and pom-pom.

Refer to Hand Template (Hand #4) for the suggested hands to use here. Pom-pom is made from a wooden bead, mounted to the hat with a 1/8" wooden dowel. After glue is dry, saw or cut the dowel flush with the outside edge of the bead.

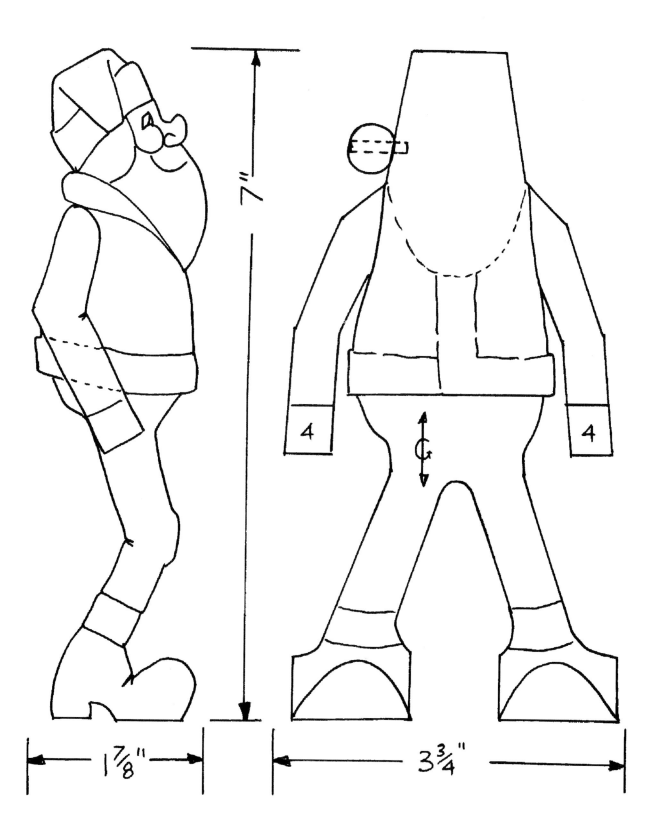

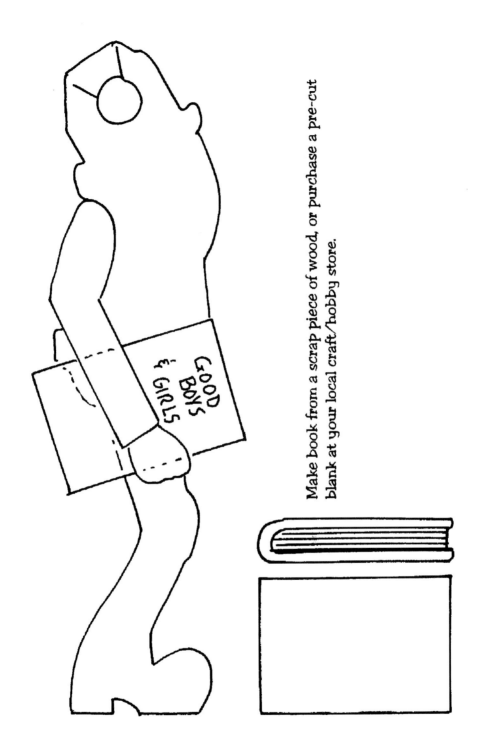

Make book from a scrap piece of wood, or purchase a pre-cut blank at your local craft/hobby store.

3¾"

8⅜"

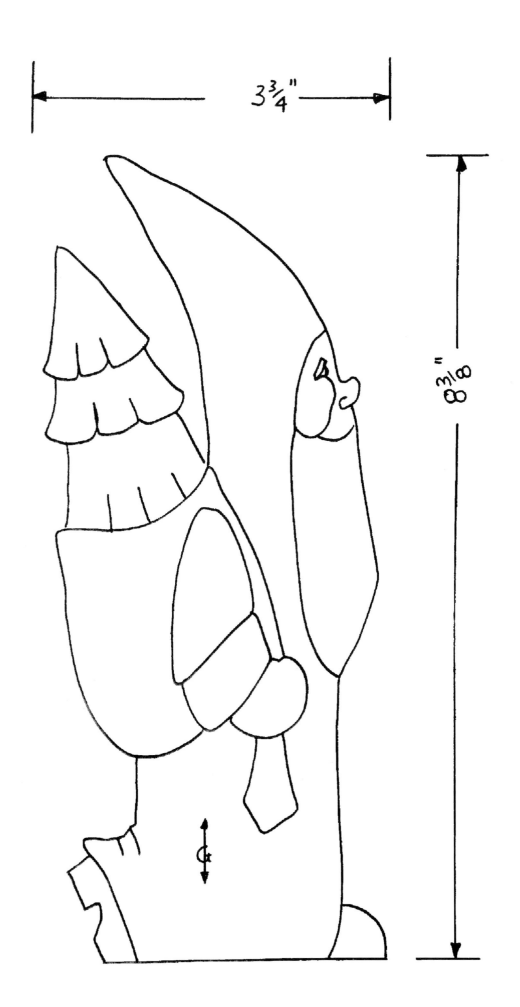

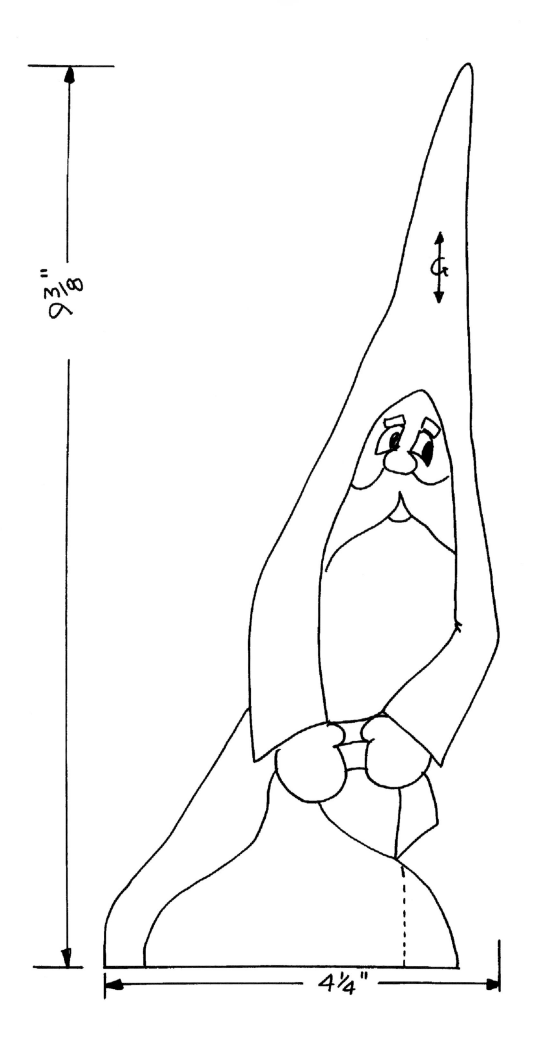

9³⁄₈"

¢

4¼"

44

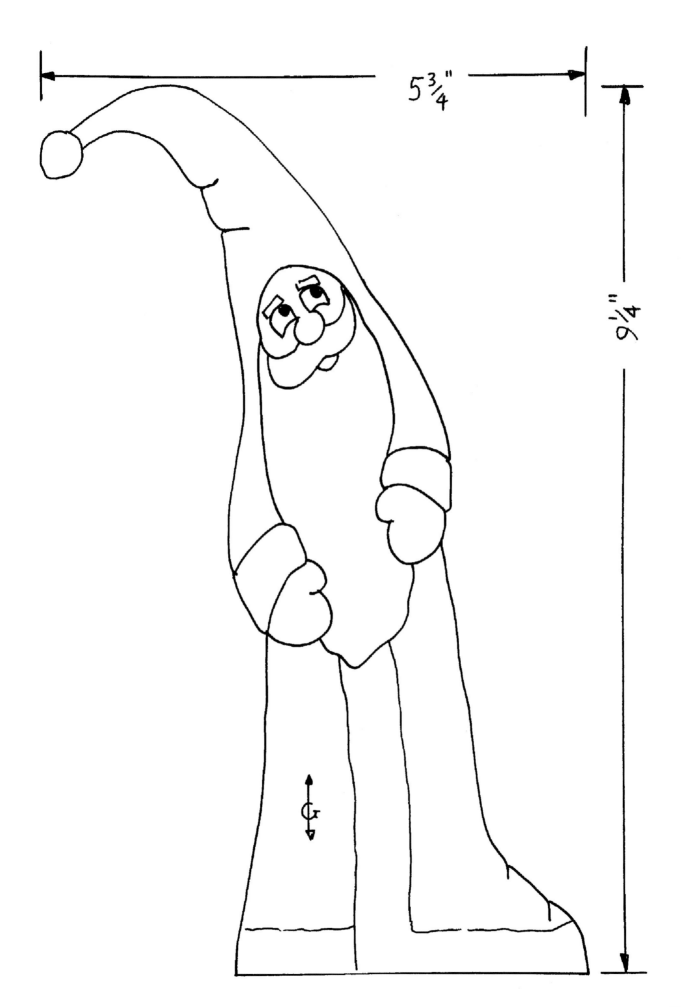

5 3/4"

9 1/4"

45

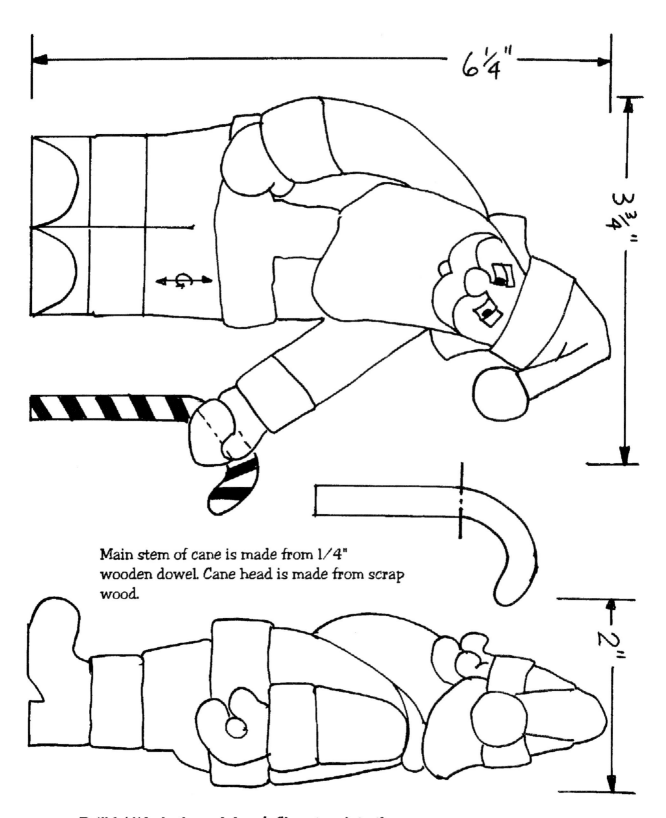

6¼"

3¾"

Main stem of cane is made from 1/4"
wooden dowel. Cane head is made from scrap
wood.

2"

Drill 1/4' hole through hand. Glue stem into the
bottom of the hand; glue the cane head into the top
of the hand.

5"

9 3/4"

3"

8"